WHAT EVERY TEAC[...]

The
Bible

Developed by the
Christian Education Staff
of The General Board of Discipleship
of The United Methodist Church

DISCIPLESHIP RESOURCES

P.O. BOX 340003 • NASHVILLE, TN 37203-0003
www.discipleshipresources.org

This booklet was developed by the Christian Education Staff of The General Board of Discipleship of The United Methodist Church. It is one in a series of booklets designed to provide essential knowledge for teachers. Members of the staff who helped write and develop this series are Terry Carty, Bill Crenshaw, Donna Gaither, Rick Gentzler, Mary Alice Gran, Susan Hay, Betsey Heavner, Diana Hynson, Carol Krau, MaryJane Pierce Norton, Deb Smith, Julia Wallace, and Linda Whited.

Cover and book design by Joey McNair
Cover illustration by Mike Drake

Edited by Debra D. Smith and David Whitworth

ISBN 0-88177-361-1

DR361

Contents

*This booklet is dedicated to
YOU,
a teacher of
children, youth, or adults,
WHO,
with fear, excitement, joy,
and commitment,
allows God to lead you
in the call to
TEACH.*

*The gifts he gave were that some would be . . .
teachers, . . . for building up the body of Christ.
(Ephesians 4:11-12)*

Introduction

In accepting the invitation to teach in your congregation, you have entered into a time of growing as a Christian while you lead others to grow along with you. Whether you are a teacher of children, youth, or adults, the Bible is basic to your teaching. We never outgrow our need to spend time with the Scriptures.

This booklet is designed to provide basic knowledge of the Bible. Depending upon your previous Bible background, this booklet may serve as a crash course in Bible basics, a reminder of things you have forgotten, or encouragement to continue in regular Bible study.

Teachers and small-group leaders are growing in faith. As teachers we pay attention to our relationships with God and with others. We seek to live our faith in our daily lives. We create safe, healthy settings for people to seek God, respond to God's grace, and find support and encouragement for living as disciples in the world.

Growing in faith (which helps us become spiritual leaders) is a life-changing experience that continues throughout life. We do not do this alone. We grow with the help of God. And we grow with the help of our congregation, which supports us by providing opportunities for learning, resources for teaching, prayer, and training.

This booklet is one of ten that will equip you for teaching. Use the entire series to reinforce your own knowledge, skills, and abilities.

Other booklets in this series are:
What Every Teacher Needs to Know About
- *Christian Heritage*
- *Classroom Environment*
- *Curriculum*
- *Faith Language*
- *Living the Faith*
- *People*
- *Teaching*
- *Theology*
- *The United Methodist Church*

The Word of God

In many congregations, after the Scripture is read the worship leader will lift the Bible and say something like, "The Word of God for the people of God," and the congregation will respond, "Thanks be to God." In these statements we acknowledge the important role that the Scriptures play in the lives of Christians.

The Bible contains a wide variety of literature, including letters, poems, hymns, and stories. However, for Christians the Bible is not a literature book or a history book or a science book. It is a book of faith and as such has an authority for our lives that is different from the authority of other important books we might read. In the Bible we find recorded the faithful witness of God's people. Through the biblical message we come to know who God is and what it means to be the people of God.

When we talk about the *Word of God* we are referring to more than just the words that make up the Bible. Through the biblical record we experience the presence of God. The biblical stories are not just stories of ancient people. As we immerse ourselves in the Scriptures we recognize ourselves in the stories and come to see God's claim on our lives.

For Personal Reflection

How does the Bible guide your life? What thoughts come to your mind when you hear the Bible referred to as the Word of God?

Use the space below for your reflections.

The Old Testament

The Bible is divided into two major sections, the Old and New Testaments. The books of the Old Testament were written before the time of Jesus. They are the Scriptures that Jesus knew. Sometimes the Old Testament is also called the Hebrew Scriptures. The Old Testament was originally written in Hebrew.

Both the Old Testament and the New Testament are collections of books. The thirty-nine books of the Old Testament fall into three general categories—the Law, the Prophets, and the Writings.

Law

The first five books of the Old Testament are called the books of the Law, the Torah, or the Pentateuch.

In these five books we find the stories of Adam and

Eve, Noah, Abraham and Sarah, Isaac and Rebekah, Jacob and Rachel, Joseph, and Moses.

Some extremely important stories that are found in these books are:

- The creation of the world.
- The flood and God's covenant with Noah to never destroy the world by water.
- God's promise to Abraham and Sarah that they will become the parents of a great nation.
- The continued growth of the Hebrew people. The twelve sons of Jacob (the grandson of Abraham and Sarah) become the founders of the twelve tribes of Israel. The family moves to Egypt, where it continues to grow and prosper.
- The enslavement of the Hebrew people in Egypt when they become so populous that they pose a political threat.
- The birth and life of Moses, who leads the Hebrew people out of slavery toward the land that God has promised.
- The giving of the Ten Commandments at Mount Sinai, after the people have left Egypt.
- The preparation to enter the Promised Land after traveling in the desert for forty years.

Prophets

Twenty-one books in the Old Testament make up the Prophets. The Prophets are not found in order in the Bible but are intermixed with books that fall in the Writings category.

In the Prophets we see the continuing story of God's people. In some of the important stories in these books,

- Joshua leads the Hebrew people into the Promised Land.
- The Hebrew tribes struggle to form a new society that is ruled by God. The leaders during this time are called judges.
- The people begin to want to be like other nations and demand a king. Saul becomes the first king of Israel.
- Saul becomes a weak king. David ascends to power as the second king of Israel.
- David's son Solomon becomes the third king of Israel. Under Solomon's leadership the Temple is built in Jerusalem.
- After Solomon's death Israel divides itself into two smaller kingdoms, Israel and Judah. A series of kings reign, many of whom fall away from God.
- Prophets warn the people of Israel and Judah that destruction will come if they do not return to God.
- The Kingdom of Israel falls to the Assyrians, and many of the people are exiled to Assyria.
- The Kingdom of Judah falls to Babylon, the Temple in Jerusalem is destroyed, and many are exiled to Babylon.

• Some of the people return from exile and begin to rebuild the Temple.

Writings

The books that are referred to as the Writings include several different types of literature. Several books in this category are poetry. Perhaps best known in this group of books is Psalms. The psalms are poems and hymns that were used in worship. Some of the Writings include wise sayings, while others tell the stories of people's experiences with God.

Some of the well-known stories, poems, and proverbs found in the writings are:

• Psalm 23. This is the psalm that has brought comfort to people throughout the ages. It begins with "The LORD is my shepherd, I shall not want."
• The story of Esther, the Jewish woman who becomes queen and through wisdom and courage is able to save her people from destruction.
• The story of Job, a man who remains faithful to God even though he experiences many tribulations.
• Proverbs 15:1, "A soft answer turns away wrath, but a harsh word stirs up anger." This is one example of the many wise sayings that are found in the Book of Proverbs.
• Ecclesiastes 3. This is the poem that begins, "For everything there is a season, and a time for every matter under heaven."

- The Song of Solomon. This is a book of love poetry.
- The story of Ruth, the non-Jewish woman who becomes the great-grandmother of King David. In Ruth 1:16 we find the well-known passage "Where you go, I will go; where you lodge, I will lodge; your people shall be my people, and your God my God."

Books of the Old Testament

Law

Genesis	Numbers
Exodus	Deuteronomy
Leviticus	

Prophets

Joshua	Amos
Judges	Obadiah
1 Samuel	Jonah
2 Samuel	Micah
1 Kings	Nahum
2 Kings	Habakkuk
Isaiah	Zephaniah
Jeremiah	Haggai
Ezekiel	Zechariah
Hosea	Malachi
Joel	

Writings

Psalms	Esther
Proverbs	Daniel
Job	Ezra
Song of Solomon	Nehemiah
Ruth	1 Chronicles
Lamentations	2 Chronicles
Ecclesiastes	

For Personal Reflection

Read several psalms from the Book of Psalms and write down the feelings these psalms evoke for you.

The New Testament

The New Testament was written after the death and resurrection of Jesus. It was originally written in Greek. There are twenty-seven books in the New Testament. They can be divided into four categories—gospels, history, letters, and revelation.

Gospels

The first four books of the New Testament (Matthew, Mark, Luke, and John) are called the Gospels. The word *gospel* means good news.

The Gospels contain the good news of Jesus Christ.

In these books we find the stories of Jesus' birth, life, death, and resurrection. We also find the stories that Jesus used when he taught his disciples and others who came to hear him. These stories are called parables. They help us to understand what God is like and how God wants us to live.

Some of the stories in the Gospels are found in only one of the books while other stories are found in more than one of the Gospels. For example, the story of the wise men visiting the baby Jesus is only found in the Gospel of Matthew, while the story of Jesus driving the money changers out of the Temple is found in all four Gospels.

History

The Acts of the Apostles was written by the same person who wrote the Gospel of Luke. Acts tells the story of the coming of the Holy Spirit and the formation of the early church after Jesus' resurrection. In this book we see how the Christian church spread from its beginnings in Jerusalem all the way to Rome. It also tells how the apostle Paul came to be a Christian.

Letters

Most of the books in the New Testament are letters that were written to various churches to offer encouragement, help with problems, and pass along Christian teaching. The letters (also called epistles) frequently talk about particular issues that were facing the church. The title of each book often gives an indication of what church the letter was originally written to. For example, the Book of Romans was written to the church at Rome. Because these letters contained important information, they were not only read aloud in the church they were sent to but also copied and passed along to other churches.

Many of the letters were written by the apostle Paul. Even though these letters are found in the middle of the New Testament they were actually the first books of the New Testament to be written.

Revelation

The Book of Revelation was written at a time when the church was being persecuted by the Roman Empire. It was dangerous to speak forthrightly about the Christian faith or to criticize the government. Much in the same way that African American slaves in the nineteenth century hid the directions for escaping in stories and songs, the Book of Revelation uses symbolic language to talk about faith. Although written during a specific time of persecution, its basic message that God reigns supreme and that Christ has the power to overcome all evil is important for Christians throughout the ages.

Books of the New Testament

Gospels

Matthew	Luke
Mark	John

History

Acts of the Apostles

Letters

Romans	Titus
1 Corinthians	Philemon
2 Corinthians	Hebrews
Galatians	James
Ephesians	1 Peter
Philippians	2 Peter
Colossians	1 John
1 Thessalonians	2 John
2 Thessalonians	3 John
1 Timothy	Jude
2 Timothy	

Revelation

Revelation

For Personal Reflection

Read the story of Jesus' resurrection in all four Gospels. What insights do you get from each story? What details had you never noticed before?

Using Your Bible

Finding a Bible Passage

Some people are good at remembering Bible references, but most of us are not. When someone says, "This is similar to what Jesus said in Luke 11:2," we don't have any idea what statement the person is referring to. But that doesn't matter, because we have been given the information we need to find the passage in the Bible.

Bibles use different size pages and different sizes of print, and there is no standard number of pages in the Bible. That is why we use a Bible reference rather than a page number when communicating where a Bible passage is found.

When locating a passage the first thing to determine is what book the passage is in. In most Bibles there is a table of contents at the beginning that lists the books in the order they are found. The Old Testament will be listed first, followed by the New Testament.

There are a few books in the Bible that have the same name. For example, there are four books in the New Testament that are all called John. The Gospel of John is referenced as John and the others are referenced as 1 John, 2 John, and 3 John. When speaking we refer to them as First John, Second John, and Third John.

Locate the book and note which page it is on. Many Bibles begin numbering the first page in the Old Testament (Genesis) with one and then begin the numbering system again with page one on the first page of the New Testament (Matthew). So it is also important to identify which Testament the book is found in.

After finding the book the passage comes from, the next step is to locate the chapter the passage is in. The chapter is indicated by the number that is listed directly after the book. Using the earlier example of Luke 11:2, we would want to find the eleventh chapter of the book of Luke.

In most Bibles the chapters are indicated at the top of each page. The beginning of the chapter is usually indicated with a large number immediately in front of the first sentence in the chapter. Each book begins with chapter one. A chapter may cover less than one page or several pages. Some books of the Bible have only one chapter and other books have many chapters.

Chapters are divided into smaller sections called verses. Verses are usually indicated by a small super-script number immediately before the first word of the verse. In a biblical reference the verse or verses follow the chapter number and are separated from the chapter number by a colon. The Bible reference Luke 11:2 means verse two of the eleventh chapter of the Book of Luke.

Sometimes a Bible reference will include a lower-case *a* or *b* after the verse number. This means that the reference includes not the entire verse but only the first half (*a*) or second half (*b*). For example, the reference Luke 11:1-4a indicates that the passage begins with verse 1 and ends with the first sentence in verse 4, at the words "indebted to us."

Luke 11

11 He was praying in a certain place, and after he had finished, one of his disciples said to him, "Lord, teach us to pray, as John taught his disciples." 2He said to them, "When you pray, say:

Father, hallowed be your name.

Your kingdom come.

3 Give us each day our daily bread.

4 And forgive us our sins,

for we ourselves forgive

everyone indebted to us.

And do not bring us to the time of trial.

Using a Concordance

If you know some of the words in a Bible passage but do not know where the passage is located, you can use a Bible reference book called a concordance to help find the passage.

A complete concordance lists all of the words in the Bible and tells you which passages include that word. For example, if you wanted to find the verse that says, "And now faith, hope, and love abide, these three; and the greatest of these is love," you could look in a concordance under the words *abide, hope, greatest,* or any of the other words in the verse to discover that this is found in 1 Corinthians 13:13. Of course if you looked under a very common word such as *these,* you would find many, many Biblical references.

Some Bibles include an abbreviated concordance. While it won't help you find every passage in the Bible, it can often help you find some of the most frequently used passages.

Excerpt From a Concordance

Greatest

Job 1:3	this man was the **greatest** of all
Mark 9:34	who was the **greatest**.
Acts 8:10	from the least to the **greatest**.
1 Cor. 13:13	the **greatest** of these is love.

Different Translations

Because neither the Old Testament nor the New Testament was originally written in English, the Bibles that we use are translations. The first English translations of the Bible were made a little more than six hundred years ago.

About four hundred years ago the translation known as the King James Version was published. It was created by a group of fifty-four translators appointed by King James I of England.

Up until 1947 the earliest known existing Hebrew manuscripts of the Old Testament came from around the ninth century A.D. Remember that before the invention of the printing press, manuscripts had to be copied by hand, a very difficult task.

However, in 1947 a shepherd boy discovered some ancient scrolls near the west shore of the Dead Sea. Over the following years more scrolls were discovered. These scrolls, which date from mid–third century B.C. to mid–first century A.D., include all of the books of the Old Testament except for the Book of Esther.

In addition, in the past two hundred years many more manuscripts of the Greek text of the New Testament have been found. Many of these manuscripts are older than those used by the King James translators, and scholars believe they provide us with a more accurate picture of the original text than was available at that time.

The discovery of the Dead Sea Scrolls and older and more numerous Greek manuscripts, as well as newer knowledge about language and word usage in Bible times, has led to a number of newer translations of the Bible. One of the most frequently used translations is the New Revised Standard Version, which was published in 1989. Other well-known translations include the New International Version and the Contemporary English Version.

Sometimes a Bible is not translated from Greek and Hebrew but is a paraphrase, a retelling of the Bible in the author's own words. Some children's Bibles are paraphrases rather than translations. A well-known paraphrase is *The Living Bible*.

For Personal Reflection

Pick one of your favorite Bible stories and read it in several translations. What new insights did you gain from the various versions?

Bible Reference
Books

In addition to a concordance, mentioned in the last section, there are several Bible reference tools that will help you explore your Bible. Remember, however, that they are just tools. Reading *about* the Bible is helpful but can never replace actually reading the Bible.

Bible Atlas

The Bible encompasses thousands of years of history. As time passed, cities rose and fell, new nations were formed, and boundaries between nations changed. A Bible atlas contains maps of Bible lands at various times in history. For example, if you wanted to know where Nazareth (Jesus' hometown) was located you would look at a map of Palestine in New Testament times. Nazareth would probably not appear on a map of the same region depicting the time of Abraham.

Sometimes you will find a simple Bible atlas at the back of your Bible. Your church library may have a more complete Bible atlas.

Bible Dictionary

Suppose that while reading your Bible you encountered the phrase from Psalm 104:26, "There go the ships, and Leviathan." Would you know what the *Leviathan* was? If not you could go to a Bible dictionary for help. Words are listed alphabetically and you look them up in the same way you look up words in a regular dictionary.

Some Bible dictionaries will give a short definition of the word you are looking up. Other Bible dictionaries will have an article that may include extensive information about the history of the word and its significance in the Bible.

You can use a Bible dictionary to look up people, places, and events.

Excerpt from a Bible Dictionary

Leviathan (li-vi-uh-thuhn)

The Leviathan is a sea serpent or a dragon. In the Bible it is sometimes used to represent chaos. It comes from a word meaning "twisting one."

Commentary

A *commentary* is a book that gives additional information about biblical passages. For example, if you were reading the story of Jesus' birth in Luke 2 and wanted to find out what biblical scholars thought about this passage, you could turn to a commentary on the Book of Luke. Usually the biblical references are listed at the top of the page. Most commentaries will describe what is happening in the passage, will provide some historical background, and will offer interpretive thoughts about the significance of the passage.

Some commentaries are written on just one book of the Bible while others cover several biblical books in one volume. At times you may want to refer to more than one commentary to get a variety of interpretations.

For Personal Reflection

Choose one of your favorite Bible stories and, after rereading it in the Bible, read a commentary on the passage. What new things did you learn about this passage?

Ways to Study
the Bible

Bible study is often referred to as a means of grace. This means that Bible study is one channel through which we experience God's love. It is a spiritual practice or discipline that helps us grow as disciples—people who love God and love their neighbors.

Sometimes we study Scripture for guidance in particular situations we are facing, sometimes we use Scripture as a way to focus and direct our prayers, sometimes we study Scripture to draw courage and understanding from faithful people of the past, and sometimes we study Scripture to learn the teachings of Jesus.

It is helpful to have an intentional regular plan for Bible study. For some this means becoming part of a Bible-study class or group. For others it means setting aside a particular time each day to engage in Bible study. There are devotional books available that will suggest a particular Scripture for each day. Some people choose a particular book of the Bible to study and work their way through it, reading a little each day. Many teachers use the Scripture that their curriculum is based on to guide their Bible-study plan.

There is not one "right" way to study the Bible. Using different methods of Bible study will help you to experience the power of the Scriptures in new ways. Following are several suggestions for Scripture study.

Use a Variety of Translations and Resources

Select a Bible passage. Read it in several different translations. Think about what the passage says. Use a Bible dictionary to help you understand any words you are unfamiliar with.

Discuss what the passage meant to the people in Bible times who originally heard it. Use other Bible reference books to help you understand what the historical and cultural conditions of the time were. Locate places mentioned in a Bible atlas.

Discuss what meaning the passage has for us today. Determine if there are changes that need to be made in your own life, based on the message of the passage.

Use Your Senses

Listen as someone reads a Bible story several times. As you listen to the story imagine that you are one of the characters in the story. Each time the story is told focus on one of your senses. What are you hearing? What are you seeing? What do you taste? What do you feel? What do you smell?

Discuss what you experienced with others.

Paraphrase the Scripture

Choose a Scripture passage and then paraphrase the passage in your own words. As you write the paraphrase think about what the Scripture means for your own life.

Illustrate the Scripture

Read a Bible passage and then paint or draw a picture that illustrates a key scene from the story. Another way to illustrate the story is to draw a picture as if the story were occurring in modern times.

Instead of actually creating a picture of the scene, you could paint or draw a picture that reflects how the passage makes you feel. Modeling clay or other media can also be used.

Keep a Journal

Each day after reading a Bible passage, reflect on the passage in a journal. Record insights you gained from the passage. Reflect on ways that your own life relates to the passage. Consider what you think God is trying to say to you through the passage.

Pray the Scriptures

Quiet your body and mind and anticipate listening for God. Read a Scripture passage or listen as someone else reads a passage aloud. Sit quietly, opening yourself to God's presence.

For Personal Reflection

Use at least two of the methods described in this section with one of your favorite Bible passages. Reflect on which method you preferred.

Going Further

The Bible is filled with powerful stories that have many layers of meaning. As we grow and mature in our faith we encounter God in new and challenging ways in old familiar passages. For example, for children the significance of the story of Jesus' birth may be that Jesus was once a child himself. As we grow older the story takes on deeper meaning and raises new questions for our lives. What does it mean that God appeared in human form? How does knowing that the Son of God was first announced to poor people change the way I relate to other people? How is the angel's message to the shepherds also a message to me?

As you become more familiar with your Bible it is likely that you will experience a thirst to drink even more deeply from the wells of its wisdom and truth.

As a teacher you may face particular challenges in finding opportunities for Bible study. Classes may be offered at the exact same time that you are teaching your own class.

However, many churches offer classes or groups at times other than Sunday morning. The DISCIPLE Bible study program is offered in many churches. It begins with a thirty-four-week study that includes both the Old and New Testaments. DISCIPLE involves daily Bible readings and a weekly class.

Some churches offer a mid-week lectionary group in which the participants study the Scripture that will be preached on in the following Sunday's worship service. A lectionary is a calendar of suggested Scripture readings. Most lectionaries include a reading from the Old Testament, a reading from the Gospels, a reading from the Epistles, and a psalm. Many pastors use *The Revised Common Lectionary* to guide worship planning. *The Revised Common Lectionary* is based on a three-year cycle. If you have ever talked with a friend whose pastor preached about the same Scripture on the same day as your pastor did, then it is likely that both pastors were preaching from the lectionary.

Sample Entry From a Lectionary

First Sunday of Advent

Year A

Old Testament	Isaiah 2:1-5
Psalm	Psalm 122
Gospel	Matthew 24:36-44
Epistle	Romans 13:11-14

Year B

Old Testament	Isaiah 64:1-9
Psalm	Psalm 80:1-7, 17-19
Gospel	Mark 13:24-37
Epistle	1 Corinthians 1:3-9

Year C

Old Testament	Jeremiah 33:14-16
Psalm	Psalm 25:1-10
Gospel	Luke 21:25-36
Epistle	1 Thessalonians 3:9-13

For Personal Reflection

Describe your plan for studying the Scriptures. What are you currently doing that you want to continue? What new things do you plan to do?

Helpful Resources

Websites

General Board of Discipleship of The United Methodist Church (www.gbod.org). On this site you will find articles related to discipleship and teaching. At www.gbod.org/worship you will find current lectionary readings.

Discipleship Resources (www.discipleshipresources.org). This is an online bookstore where you can purchase additional copies of this booklet, other booklets in the series, and other books from Discipleship Resources.

Books

The Anchor Bible Dictionary, edited by David Noel Freedman (Doubleday, 1992). A six-volume Bible dictionary. It includes articles on thousands of topics related to the Bible.

The Concise Concordance to the New Revised Standard Version, edited by John R. Kohlenberger III (Oxford University Press, 1993). A helpful concordance to the most important words in the New Revised Standard Version of the Bible.

The HarperCollins Bible Pronunciation Guide, edited by William O. Walker Jr (HarperCollins, 1984). Provides the pronunciation for more than seven thousand names and other words found in the Bible.

The New Oxford Annotated Bible, New Revised Standard Version, edited by Bruce M. Metzger and Roland E. Murphy (Oxford University Press, 1994). A study Bible that includes informational footnotes, cross-references, Bible maps, an abbreviated concordance, and other study helps.

Oxford Bible Atlas, edited by Herbert G. May (Oxford University Press, 1984). Includes maps and photographs of biblical sites.

The Revised Common Lectionary, by the Consultation on Common Texts (Abingdon, 1992).

The Spiritual Formation Bible, edited by Timothy Jones (Zondervan, 1999). Available in both the New Revised Standard Version and the New International Version. Includes devotional helps.